We the people

Poems by

PHILLIP LARREA

Other titles by Phillip Larrea:
Our Patch (published by Writing Knights Press, 2013)

Cover Design by Bodhi

Photograph of Homeless Man © Matthew Woitunski

Illustration of Thomas Jefferson inspired by
        Rembrandt Peale (1778–1860)

Photograph of Times Square © Terrabass

ISBN: 978-0-9846403-6-2

Library Of Congress Control Number: 2013935134

A PRIMAL URGE PUBLICATION

printed by
Cold River Press
102 S. Church Street
Grass Valley, CA 95945

www.coldriverpress.org

Preface

What about the quietly desperate?

No food drives, star-studded fundraisers or charitable foundations for these. We have met the characters in this book. They are us.

Dedication

Special thanks to the poets and editors who have been a source of inspiration and encouragement during the process of writing these poems.

Pamela Clarke Vandall, Sharon Frye, Jt Odochartaigh, Brendan McCormack, Silva Merjanian, Gene Barry, Peadar O'Donoghue, Micheal Gallagher, FP Kenny, Bill Gainer, Laura Martin, Linda Collins, Karin Erickson, David Iribarne, Mike and Eva West, Dr. Andy Jones, Bob Stanley, Tim Kahl, Emmanuel Ilgauke, Allegra Silberstein, Eva Xanthopoulos, Azriel Johnson and many more.

Most of all, my thanks to Dave Boles, editor of Primal Urge and Cold River Press for believing in this work. Dave Boles does not merely talk the talk ~ he is that rare soul who walks the walk.

Thank you all

Foreword

The need to express our beliefs, our observations, our feelings towards the world at large, is a primal force within us all. Though some may have a more accelerated desire towards expression than others, the need for this expression exists nonetheless. It is exactly this need that connects the poet, the writer, the artist, with their audience. Not only is there a need to be heard, but there is also a deep desire to hear as well.

Phillip Larrea, possesses the rare ability to focus, succinctly, his message, his expression, onto the printed page for all to read and hear. His ability to weave a message with the use of short, concise poems is an accomplishment few can master, and indeed he is a master at using language to drive straight to the point. His vivid expressions come as varied as his poetry; they range from love poems that stir the heart to political diatribes that expose the malicious renderings of our corrupt leaders and officials. He manages to accurately describe a wide host of human conditions and poignantly attends to these conditions with the nurturing care that only a skilled wordsmith can muster.

It is in his role as a skilled wordsmith that he takes to heart the task of the poet who not only is compelled to write upon the world as he sees it, but to write about the political subjugation and oppression about him. Larrea writes in an effort to reach out to others, to let them know they are not alone. Where other poets in our current day are quick to shy away from such malodorous matters, Phillip deftly combines his talents and use of language to expose these traitorous bastards for what they are and leaves no doubt as to the poverty and enslavement they lead us to. His offerings provide succinct curtailment to these dishonorable and vicious curs.

In his opening lines he writes, "What about the quietly desperate?" Indeed, what about them? Who will speak for them? Have they no voice at all? When our forefathers crafted this country they did so with the intent that all of its citizens would be free from the tyranny of government, not just a handful of wealthy and prosperous citizens, but every citizen from every level of our political and economic landscape. Thomas Jefferson, Benjamin Franklin, Thomas Payne, et al... sought to protect our freedoms from being usurped by political leaders that would feed the bloated machinations of their failed government with the suffering of its citizenry. For those "quietly desperate" amongst us, and their ranks grow larger with every passing day, Phillip Larrea offers a voice, an island of consciousness amid an ever increasing tide of immoral rapists and plunderers that flourish in these troubled times. He reminds us of our humanity; to not become lost. Though we may be adrift, there is still the semblance of hope, there is still the slightest flicker of freedom for all.

Phillip's manuscript is one of the rare literary gems that stands out from the rest. Rarely does a manuscript speak with such clarity. The existential nature of Phillip Larrea's writing touches us all and reminds us of the connection we share as travelers in this brief period of time. It is an honor to be connected with, and to publish this work.

"We The People"....how appropriate.

Table Of Contents

Arrested..17

Wrong, Right And Reasonable.....................20

Lord's Player...22

Suitcase In Hand...................................23

Chess Game...24

You Don't Care.......................................25

What She Saw There................................26

The Complete Walt Whitman....................27

Toothpaste Man......................................27

Twinkie Forever......................................28

Ruling Class...29

Lake Tahoe, 2004....................................30

Killer Mind..31

Imposters...32

Halloween..33

Hard Child...34

Fascination...35

Closing Time..36

Death March..38

Cliches..39

Letter from Thomas Jefferson to
    John "the Tory" Randolph-Aug. 1775.......40

Cardinal Sins..41

Homecoming..42

Off The Cliff..43

Table Of Contents

So Unfair..44

No Team In I..45

Wins And Losses..46

The Bartender..47

Night Ferry..48

Gatekeepers..49

Bank Owned...50

Cure For Health...51

My Valediction...52

Irishness...54

Stiff..55

Scrapbook Villanelle.....................................56

The Edge..57

Zen Koan...58

Last Butterfly..59

Reincarnation...60

Samurai Haiku..61

Slipping Away...62

Locke's Box..63

The Punch Line or
     Things Are Not As They Seem.................64

Elegy For Eliot...66

Just A Few Dollars More...............................68

Falling Time...69

Author Bio...71

Acknowledgements.......................................73

Arrested

Patriots of the One Nation Brigade
Filed up our walkway. My wife turned to me,
      "Aaron- what have you done?"
      "It could be anything."
The man with chevroned sleeves indicating
His insignia as an Important
One, stepped forward.
      "Aaron Swartz? You must come
With me."
      "I am an Aaron Swartz. Surely
Not the Aaron Swartz you are looking for.
Of what am I accused?"
      "Wickard v. Filburn.
Sir, we have aerial surveillance photos
Which show that you have grown wheat with intent,
We believe, to consume. Were you aware
That this is a serious crime against
One Nation? Doesn't matter. We do not
Excuse ignorance."
      "Wheat? A crime? This can't
Be true. In any case, I wouldn't even
Know how to do such a thing. I swear, I
Have never so much as seen a wheat stalk."
      "Then explain this." He slammed a photo down.

"What? That whippoorwill?"

"Oh, I think you know

Very well, this is no whippoorwill. Wheat!

Wheat with intent to consume!"

"What of it?

Not a serious crime, I hope. How much

Is the fine?"

"Not serious? You might as

Well have planted a bomb at the National

Wheat Production Facility. Do you

Not understand that you have threatened the

Lives, livelihood and security of

Every citizen of One Nation?

Under the powers vested in me by

Authority to Act in the National

Defense, you, Aaron Swartz, are now under

Arrest. You do not have the right to an

Attorney, nor will one be allowed to

Represent you. You do not have the right

To a trial, nor will one be conducted

On your behalf. Do you understand these

Restrictions as I have read them to you?"

"Wait, wait." My wife cried out. "I have
something. Here. See here, this Bible. From the
eighteenth century. Look. Look inside. Signed by
John Adams, himself. He took the oath on this
Bible. You can have it. Take it. As bail.

Not a bribe, you understand. A fine, yes?
Let us confess we broke a law, and will
Pay the fine."

"A Bible? Put that away.
Comrade, please note for the record, Ms. Swartz
Offered an antique book ~ do not say what
Kind ~ as collateral for this man's bail."

As they hauled me away by the elbows,
Important One turned to my wife and, in
Sotto voce said, 'Do not show that book
To anyone, ever again. We of
One Nation, pledge allegiance to our god."

Wrong, Right and Reasonable
(Adapted from an essay by Benjamin Franklin, 1767)

It is Wrong, O ye Americans, for you to expect hereafter

That we will make any acts of Congress from the time we,

The Gentle Shepherd and his flock get into power but
   such

As are calculated to impoverish you ~ and enrich us.

Our standing maxim is, you exist only for our sakes.

Your Lords we are, and slaves we deem ye.

It is Right to call this by the name "bounty".

We express our Goodness to you more clearly to intimate
   the

Great Obligation you are under for such Goodness.

Yet ~ you manifest the ungratefulness of your tempers by
   objecting,

In return for such Goodness, to take upon yourselves

A burden ten hundred times greater than the bounty!

It is Reasonable, O ye Americans, to charge you with
   dreaming,

Otherwise we cannot keep you so poor, but you may pay
   your debt,

Dreaming that you may encrease your own strength and
   prosperity.

Joseph's brethren hated him for a dream he really
dreamed.
We, for a dream you never dreamed, which we only
dream
You dreamed, have therefore resolved to hate you most
  cordially.

Lord's Player *

Often times, I am stuck sitting
For hours and hours on end
In between meetings
On which the day's success depends.

Some odd spot, no amenities.
Maybe a coffee
In a parking lot
Descending to serenity.

This ridiculous pilgrimage
Not between temples dark.
More like an amusement park where
Madcap harlequins pillage plots.

She asks, "How did it go today?"
"Oh, fine... bad... okay."
The best part, I can't really say,
Was spent in the Lord's field ~ at play.

* from the title "At Play in the Fields of the Lord"
by Peter Mathiessen

Suitcase in Hand

Cold in the hours between
Late last night
Not yet tomorrow
Suitcase in hand.

Door stands halfway open
Day tips, hangs
In the balance.

Chess Game

A chess match.
Since you're white,
You move first.

Knights, castle,
Queen lost. King
Checkmated.

No deaths here.
Just pieces
Of me gone.

You Don't Care

Have mercy!
Please God ~ no
Hop-head highs

Creamy thighs
Winds that sigh
When love dies.

You don't care
That I care
If you don't.

What She Saw There

"High in cerulean skies, weeps the statue..."
She had been on summer sabbatical
To Sao Paolo was it, I think she said?
No, no ~ now I recollect it was Rio.
She shows snapshots from her trip. Heartfelt captions
Using literate words seldom heard ever.
We display our profound appreciation
With golf claps. Her colleague in the back row
Snaps his fingers. The adjunct on the side
Nods, eyes closed, deeply entranced, no doubt.
Next, she anaconds us down Amazon
Pleistocene rainforests. We smell compost.
Last ~ an ekphrastic of empty pottery.
Smash show! We defenestrate such poetry.

The Complete Walt Whitman
~ a haiku

I am beautiful.
Everyone else too. But
Me more so than you.

Toothpaste Man ~ Haiku

Famous toothpaste man
Squeezed from bottom to top, then
Gets his head lopped off.

Twinkie Forever

The twinkie
Has taught us
A half-life

Is longer
Than a full.
When you pray,

Skip the saints.
"Preserve us,
Monsanto!"

Ruling Class

It is the great misfortune of my life
To be named Aaron, instead of Zyloff.
My assigned desk always in the front row,
My address closest to Headmaster's station.
Not like Zyloff, who gets to sit in back
Where we all want to hide, making mischief.
Hardly ever called for the right answer.
Last brought to order, first one out the door.

Isn't easy keeping the peace, I know
Classes are large. There must be rules, surely
(Arbitrarily applied, seems to me)
So Headmaster can rule the unruly.
Still ~ I think I am no worse than Zyloff,
Just pure bad luck, first stung by the ruler.

Lake Tahoe, 2004

Violin
Old vine twist
Reminisce

Piano
Naughty pine
Wine sins then

Saxophone
Flight willow
Antique bind

Killer Mind

Killer mind
Profiled ill
Since third grade.

No permits
To work here.
'Go west', gone.

Unsexy
Sick bastard.
We'll fix him.

Imposters

This bearded Beat peered at me
dubiously through the Prohibition
basement speakeasy peephole.
I slid my bona fides through.

I wore my funky duck flapped
knit cap with strings I bought
to hide my full head of hair.
Ditched my crimson class tie in the Lex.

He kept looking me down, then up.
Puffy eyes flicking back and forth.
"This ain't gonna fly," I thought.
Like that instant in an arm wrestle
when you know you are bound to lose.

Then he caught the smoke in my hand.
Maybe my cherry deflected off his bald dome.

"Hell, c'mon in kid. One or two of your kind
won't kill us, I guess. Dying breed anyhow..
Can't stomach the bourbon or
silver spoon reflections anymore.
All smoke and mirrors, baby.
Mostly smoke."

Halloween

She wore a revealing
Vampire slut zombie number.
He was resplendent in the full
Marilyn, from wig down to the bone.
Other days they wear costumes.

Hard Child

Make you a hard child.
One who can taste their own sweat
In morning, evening meals.

Palms thick enough to grip an ax.
Fingers slender to thread needles,
Or pull a trigger.

Give them a gun,
Then show them death up close.
Make you a hard child, yet

Do not forget they are but children
To be protected at all cost, by any means,
From the uniform.

Fascination

Fully~clothed
Women do
Allure just

As men wrapped
Deep in thought
Fascinate.

Nakedness
Is best viewed
Dimly lit.

Closing Time

I leave some paper on the bar.
Thank my Host for a pretty good time.
All work for Him, I know.
I pretend we are on good terms, nonetheless.

Most of my fellow revelers have left.
I don't know where they go
when they are not here.
Doesn't much matter, I suppose.

Tonight, the home team has staged an upset
against all the bookmakers' odds.
A rebound from last week's crushing defeat.
I collect my winnings, buy Jack Daniels all around.

This earns me a dance and squeeze
from that pretty young thing
who drops by every now and again.
She has the good sense to leave early though.

I'm ruddy. The game is in the books.
A bit of pinch and tickle.
I'm old enough to know
this is as good as it gets.

The Man gives me that look now.
Like it's time to close up shop.
Outside, I find I still have scrip in my pocket.
I wish I had left it all on the bar.

Death March

Life is a
death march, so
we drag feet.

She prays to
her Lover,
but the end

is The End.
I light a
cigarette.

Cliches

Tongue quiver
Slippery
Gaze chills hard

Fingertips
Explode moist
Bud chocolate

Shiver hot
Crave creamy
Moon shattered.

Letter from Thomas Jefferson to
John "the Tory" Randolph ~ Aug. 1775
A Revolutionary Poem

Dear Sir ~ As to the violin left here in haste
Upon your urgent departure from our harbor;
I am sorry that our country's situation
Should render you no longer able to remain.
Though she is presently ill~tuned, and lacks a case,
I shall, with my utmost care, preserve her safety.

Upon arrival to your seat of government,
Please convey to your Ministry, this American
Opposition is no small faction, as believed.
They have taken into their heads, we are cowards,
And will surrender to an armed force. They are wrong.
This I affirm, and place my honour upon it.

If it be within your power to undeceive
On this point, at this critical time, you perform
Such service to nations, as the world has not seen.
They must hold out no false hope, no ignorance of
Our real intentions. Rather than submit, I would
Lend my hand to sink the whole island in the ocean.

40

Cardinal Sins

Venal cheek
Windshield crack
Spider web

Bulbous nose
Mass shamans
Peddle wares.

Refurbished
Body parts
Sold cheap here.

Homecoming

Come winter,
We come home.
Where it's warm.

Or gone cold.
As a hearth
Smoldering.

Blood thicker
Than water.
Dried hard ~ stone.

Off the Cliff

The path is lush and green,
Slopes gently upward to the cliff.
In the far off distance, crashing waves
Sound as soft as the sirens' songs.

But the final few strides
Are stony hard with cuts.
Below, hopes against the rocks, dashed.
Falling ~ til the end ~
Feels like flying.

So Unfair

So unfair
That something
In water

Or the air
Or sunlight
Or beauty

Or the pills
Or their men ~
Kills women.

No Team in I

I was on a team once.
We had uniforms.
We had equipment.
We sure as heck kept score.

We didn't like each other much.
The best player whined a lot.
The consistent ones fumed.
And damn those who saved their best for last.

We won most of the time.
May I say, none too graciously.
We behaved despicably in defeat.
We had what is known as 'team chemistry'.

I wasn't happy then but,
I love my trophy now.
I savor my immutable victory and gloat.
There is no team in I.

Wins and Losses

We were ripped
From high school
Sports pages.

Heroin.
Feeling? No.
Pain, no gain.

We had game.
Seeing stars.
Not no more.

The Bartender

"Gin and tonic please,"
He says to me.
Though I know it well
By his dollars that flutter
Like fallen leaves to my gutter,
That trough we 'tenders call "the well".

This glass before me like his brain.
Ice cubes the cells that remain
With gaps good Gordon fills.
Tonic that whispers and bubbles;
Jokes making light of his troubles ~
While I keep an eye on his bills.

Night Ferry

To die from the wound, or live with the scar,
We are the maimed, we fill your bars.
Know the cripple by the crutch he carries,
Hobbling aboard the night ferry.

We've got places to be, nowhere to go,
Huddling, singing, "swing low…"
We have to live because we cannot die;
Not for some jackdaw reason why
That calms our muscle memory twitches ~
No flesh to balm where it itches.

Gatekeepers

Gatekeepers.
Sclerotic
Congealed sludge.

They defend
Til their death
Vain puff fish.

Poor sad sacks.
Detritus.
Bottom rot.

Bank Owned

Seize my home?
Sell me short?
Foreclosure.

Two bedrooms,
one bathroom.
And a dog.

Property
is bank owned.
Always was.

Cure For Health

Doc Sawbones
Says to me,
"Such good health ~

Despite your
Bad habits.
Just for that ~

I'll kill you
More slowly
Than usual."

My Valediction

"We are NOT at the crossroads of life…"
So, in truth, my valediction began.
Not quite the speech the Administration had planned.

In fact, I should ~ would ~ have been expelled days ago,
For putting my drunken fist through the bathroom stall,
Except that the stoned-in-class president was already
gone.

Which is how I came to stand for the best
This small country had to offer. My last words were,
"Farewell. I hope I never see most of you again."

Thus I took my leave, severed ties, declared indepen-
dence.
"A speech they will not forget," I thought. But they did.
That fist mark though, remains to this very day.

I know it is so, because we reunited years later.
Bald chums all made jolly with "hullo, how have you
been?"
And, "What did you become? A leader of men, I bet."

"Oh, no," I incline my head with acquired humility,
"Upon sober reflection, I thought it best, in truth
To drink, clench my fists, and punch holes in bathroom
stalls."

Irishness

Irish cannot be governed,
Not even by himself.
A dark, dark place it is.
Black as the final draft,
The last laugh at closing time…
As what happens later.

Irish ~ that lyric floating through ether
Before the pitiless surgeon's blade
Slices into your bowels up the gut
To get at your faulty heart valve.

"Good fortune" seldom follows "Irish".
Worse the luck when it does.

So don't you believe them stories
About Emerald Isle faeries.
Irish, thick druid copse, alright.
Leaves an indelible scar.
Suppressed, never tamed.
Tempting as hemlock
To a starving soul.

Stiff

Here I was
Several
Lifetimes back.

And back here,
Someone else.
Different.

Colder face.
Harsh climate
Stiffening.

Scrapbook Villanelle

The plot of my life is a book of scraps.
Discovered, it seems, by another's hand.
The path becomes clear by reading the map.

Memory is short, and many the gaps.
Often, I hardly recognize the land.
The plot, my life, is in a book of scraps.

This moment can jar like a thunderclap.
Then absorbed by the rest ~ rain into sand.
The path becomes clear by reading the map.

My fingers fumble like a blind cane taps.
Groping for direction, some common band,
Within the plot of my life's book of scraps.

On now and then, tomorrow overlaps.
Pushing in directions I had not planned.
The path becomes clear by reading the map.

One day, it may all crystallize, perhaps.
Action, purpose, fused by waving a wand.
The plot of my life is a book of scraps.
The path becomes clear by reading the map.

The Edge

No tricks of the trade,
No unfair advantage.
No edge in experience,
No wisdom hollow.

To simply go
To a place they know
You have gone,
But no one can follow.

Zen Koan

Mea culpa
Mea culpa
Mea maxima culpa.

Of course, it is my fault.
Who else should it be.

How shall I blame You, Lord?
You were not even there at the time.

Last Butterfly

Surely the last person you would expect
To exterminate a species.

To know so much, understand so little,
Was not for lack of study.

"Such a shame," he thought, "that this lepid
Is so rarely seen in cities."

Collateral damage at most, to pin just one
For the benefit of posterity.

Who would have thought this one
Was the source of all others?

That this sole death, would kill them all.
Love murdered the last butterfly.

Reincarnation

Reincarnation?
Sure, why not?

I have had many lives.
Died each and every time.

That's just how it goes.
Makes for good stories though.

Samurai Haiku

Dawn of my birthday.
The Spring pushes me harder ~
Surging to the Fall.

Slipping Away

Hold on. Hold.
Fading edge
Dusk or dawn.

A moment
Or lifetime
Slips away

From the quay…
Harbor's bay…
To the deep.

Locke's Box

I plan on
Being dead.
Just prudent.

Money burns,
So I keep
My good stuff

In Locke's box.
Not worth much,
But sturdy.

The Punch Line, or
Things are not as they Seem

You cannot recover the past.
Neither can you make it last.
It fades away like the hill you climbed
To face the mountain behind.

Youth, the constant butt of a practical joke,
Face flaming red with frustration
Stands before the placid, cold magistrate
Who says, "You'll be alright son.
Things are not as they seem."

Things are not as they seem?
Suddenly with your own eyes you see
That black and white are not colors, it seems.
That time's arrow is a slingshot string
(or some such thing).

So, with uncertain, stumbling steps,
Led by a misty, distracted mind,
You come upon your own headstone.
In granite engraved the old punch line:
"Things are not as they seem

Things are as they seem."

But you cannot recall the past
You can barely even remember.
As I consider this in an afterglow ~
It is the saddest fact of life I know.

Elegy for Eliot

Who will embrace this orphan, Eliot?
He wanders certain half-deserted streets,
His nose pressed against the fogged window pane,
On the inside looking out. Longing to
Walk among the bustling half-dead throngs
Commuting from Michaelangelo there,
Crossing Renoir's bridge to Dada End.

On this bitter April Thursday morning,
He scatters remains of last night's ashes,
Tucks his practical cat in his rucksack,
Hopes to fall in with pilgrims' progress
In peace to Buddha's shrine, without a prayer.
His cross to bear ~ he does not understand.

Doubting Thomas shakes frost off his shoulders,
Wishing to crawl back into the Blessed
Mother Mary's virgin womb. But she who
Comforts each to each, will not comfort him.

He grows old ~ cast to the side of the road.
Hollowed out by every pound of flesh
Exacted by critics' ragged claws which
Damn him with faint praise, assent with a leer.

Re-baptized in the water faith, he dies.
Gasping the last air not yet consumed by fire.
A bit of earth marks his passing this way
With all that there really is left to say:
T.S. Eliot begins and ends.
Here, like a struck match, he begins again.

Just a Few Dollars More

For lack of a paltry hundred billion
Cities will burn while we stand waterless.
Thousands of civilians will lose their jobs
Straddling missiles for the military.

Millions of feral kiddie cats-unspayed,
Not medicated, will pour from cages
With no one to care for, or feed them lunch.
Just as well, snack would likely be poisoned.

Let me state plainly what this really means -
Pretty much a zombie apocalypse.
And all completely unnecessary.
A tragedy so simple to avoid.

When, with just a mere one hundred billion more,
Our man soothes us, order could be restored.

Falling Time

A feeling like water
Rushing through rusty pipes.
Cracking iron,
Seeping through sidewalks,
Buckling pavement
Carrying away street signs,
Short-circuiting stoplights,
Vanquishing venerable institutions.

Yet, I am safe.
Magically half transformed
Into some water creature,
Diving, swimming, dancing, singing
Within confusion.
Still, I am myself - perhaps more.

Night falls on my submerged city.
Amidst eddy, current, tide, torrent,
Everything fixed swept away.
One tall tower stands
Aglow in the full moon halo.

© berns photography

Phillip Larrea is the editor of "minutedots" investment newsletter, a syndicated columnist and has been a widely published poet in the U.S., U.K. and Eastern Europe. He counts Robert Frost, Mark Twain, T.S. Eliot and D.H. Lawrence as his most important modern literary influences. All of these writers share that quality of being as interesting for what they don't say, as for what they do say; how Eliot expands his text with allusion; how Lawrence evokes the interior monologue; the secular rage behind Twain's humor in his book, Letters from the Earth. No one has influenced Phillip Larrea's poetry more than Robert Frost, however. Not the Frost of "Stopping by Woods...," or "Road Not Taken", but rather, the "Dust of Snow" Frost. This poem in particular, inspired the original short form Phillip Larrea calls a 'TriCube'- many examples of which you will find in this book. The mathematical precision of these poems have their roots in "Dust of Snow". Finally, as Archibald MacLeish once wrote, "A poem should not mean, but be." The author is thrilled that this book has come into 'being'.

Acknowledgements

The author gratefully acknowledges the following publications in which many of these poems have previously appeared:

No Team In I: *Nazar Look, Outburst Magazine, The Rusty Nail*

Lord's Player: *Diogen Magazine, Nazar Look, Decades Review, Fresh Peaches (Sacramento Poetry Center Anthology)*

Bartender: *Poetry Bus Magazine, Commonline Journal, Nazar Look*

My Valediction: *Van Gogh's Ear, Outburst Magazine*

Letter from Thomas Jefferson: *Counterpunch, Our Patch (Writing Knights Press)*

Ruler Class: *Brooklyn Voice (as, St. Finbar)*

Irishness: *Outburst Magazine*

Chess Game: *Medusa's Kitchen, Nostrovia!*

Punch Line: *Sacramento Poetry Art & Music (SPAM)*

Homecoming: *Squire Anthology, The Artistic Muse*

Comp. Walt Whtman: *Four and Twenty Poetry*

Last Butterfly: *Solstice Initiative*

Locke's Box: *Possibility Place*

Killer Mind, Wrong, Right and Reasonable, What She Saw There: *Primal Urge*

Phillip Larrea has crafted a diverse and succulent meal of poetry for us inside these pages. In *Night Ferry* he adds a quiet desperation to the personified push and pull of everyday living. *Halloween* lends insight into the depths of the human psyche, a deft word painting of the masks we show the world and the ones we don't. Larrea moves into form poetry in *Scrapbook Villanelle*, a wonderful write that brings to mind Robbie Burns musings in "To A Mouse": "The best-laid schemes o' mice an' men gang aft agley."

Suitcase In Hand is a successful exercise in brevity– short and succinct yet says it all in 7 simple but powerful lines that describe everyone's life at some point in time. *Death March* is a compact portrayal of the ineffectual meaning of life in the grand scheme of things showing us the best results in living occur when it is casually dealt with.

My personal favorite is *The Punch Line*. Larrea's depth of talent shines brilliantly through in this cleverly crafted poem. It begs a second and third read, each one savoured a little more each time.

This is an evocative and commendable offering from Phillip Larrea and a very welcome addition to my "favorites" bookshelf.

Candice James,
Poet Laureate, City of New Westminster
BC CANADA

'We The People' is the second collection of poetry from Phillip Larrea. In his foreword he asks us to consider the 'quietly desperate' and acknowledge that 'They are us.' This though is not a collection of political but more a collection of deeply humanitarian poems that name the freedoms denied, the genesis of corruption at the heart of the American Dream and the consequences for a people caught within this modern day Kafkaesque trial. The first poem 'Arrested' stops us in our tracks with iambic meter punching out the insanities inherent in the recent 'Aaron Swartz' case and its echo's in earlier cases of the Government bypassing the people in order to Govern itself apart. He uses Haiku, Tricubes (an invention all his own) and sonnets to unleash his own particular brand of cutting insight leavened with a wry humour and profound sensibility that through the course of his collection allows one to begin to see the implications of a society drowning in enforced and inhumane uniformities.

In the midst, the poet finds amongst the business of life 'a parking lot / descending to serenity.' Other times he captures moments that stand still like Hopper's paintings , 'Door stands halfway open / Day tips, hangs / In the balance.' Moments that echo the tragedy of American history, 'Knights, castle / Queen lost. King / Checkmated.' We hear the voices of hipsters, of beats, of Zen masters, of Thomas Jefferson and Benjamin Franklin. We come to hear the voice amongst the multitude of sins visited upon this strange and wonderful land. We hear of his Irishness, 'Tempting as hemlock / To a starving soul.' He reminds us of thinkers who may have lit better ways. 'In Locke's box / Not worth much, /But sturdy.'

In the end it is the art of his work that illuminates everything else. His sure sense of meter and rhyme, his careful shepherding of his words through so many voices. In the end he invokes T. S. Eliot and offers his own declaration: 'T. S. Eliot begins and ends. / Here, like a struck match, he begins again.'

To get a sense of America today, this indeed would be a fine starting point.

Brendan McCormack,
Poet/Writer
Dublin, Ireland

"Phillip Larrea encourages thought in his readers and excellence in his friends. This is his most pernicious fault. From his Frost inspired and Zen-like tricubes, to his darkly humorous *Letter from Thomas Jefferson*, Phillip Larrea gives poetic variety a facelift. For my money, any poet who can use the word ekphrastic (What She Saw There) must be either incredibly erudite or crazy. Phillip Larrea may be both."

Jt Odochartaigh,
Poet/Writer
Placerville, CA

Phillip Larrea walks the literary waters. On top. (Not like that "Weekend at Bernie's" character.)

Phillip Larrea is the man to turn a poem into an artful lesson about the world: the world of revolutions, the world of torched economies, the world of the past becoming the present. He is the how-we-got-in-this-mess poet. Phillip turns an artful phrase, manipulates an allegory, and somehow begets the fluttery butterfly in China that becomes the hurricane in your backyard. Not a bad trick for a poet.

He is also the writer to make you laugh, and as you do laugh, you puzzle for the moment with, "wait a minute...did he mean what I think he means there?"

You buy the words on the page, but you get the twinkle in his eyes.

Evan Myquest
Poet/Writer
Sacramento, CA